Della and Her Garden of Flowers

Written and Illustrated by
Kathleen L. Beirne

Dedication

I dedicate this book to my 95-year-old mother, Della Rae Goss. She has given me consistent love and inspiration. And for her love of elephants and her garden of flowers. But most of all, just being you. Thank you. I love you Mom!

Copyright © 2023
All Rights Reserved

About the Author

Kathleen L. Beirne is originally from Pennsylvania. She is retired and living in Florida with her wonderful husband, Joe. Together they have six children and eleven grandchildren. She has enjoyed writing poetry for the past 20 years. Art has always been her creative ability, like sculpting, drawing, and painting. Occasionally she plays the guitar for fun. Listening to music sets the mood for relaxation. She enjoys the outdoors and traveling in their RV with her husband. Writing a children's book has always been something she wanted to do. She had a dream of a white baby elephant. It is as if someone was saying, "Now take it and run with it." So she took her dream and started writing. Her 95-year-old mother inspired her because of her love for elephants and her flower garden. Being the first book she had written, she took the challenge of drawing the illustrations. When she isn't creating, she's traveling with her husband in their RV, having new adventures.

Everyday Della walks in her garden of flowers.

Even though it made Della sneeze.

She was careful not to sniff any bumblebees.

Many of the flowers have a delightful fragrance.
Delicate and full of her numerous favorites.

Snapdragons, irises, lilies, daffodils and more.
Bright colors, all shapes and sizes galore.

The flowers are colorful and beautiful to see.
Feeling tired, Della naps under a big, big tree.

She dreams of looking like colorful flowers.
As if she has great big magical powers.

Or like a beautiful rainbow.

To her surprise, she is feeling jolly joys!
She heard a loud, fast buzzing noise.

A bumblebee had landed upon her trunk.
Now she has color with lots of spunk.

If you look closely, who do you see?
So colorful, so cheerful, so free.

It is Della dancing in her garden of flowers.
There she dances for a couple of hours.

Suddenly, Della awoke from her short nap.
Happy to have a nice dream like that.

If only her dreams and wishes would grow.
But as you see, she is the color of snow.

Near the pond at most days end.
There is Millie the turtle, Della's friend.

Eager, Della told her dream to Millie.
Millie chuckled and thought, that is just silly.

Millie looked at herself and tried to imagine.
What she would look like with colors of fashion.

Della asked Millie to close her eyes.
And try to imagine that she's made of a color surprise.

Then Della covered Millie with quite a few flowers.

They said their happy goodbyes today.
Della went on her separate way.

Sometimes Della would lay in the tall grass.
And eat a snack of greens she could not pass.

Her favorite thing is to look up at the sky.
And watch the fluffy clouds go rolling by.

She headed home through the meadow.
Excited, Della could not wait for her mother to know!

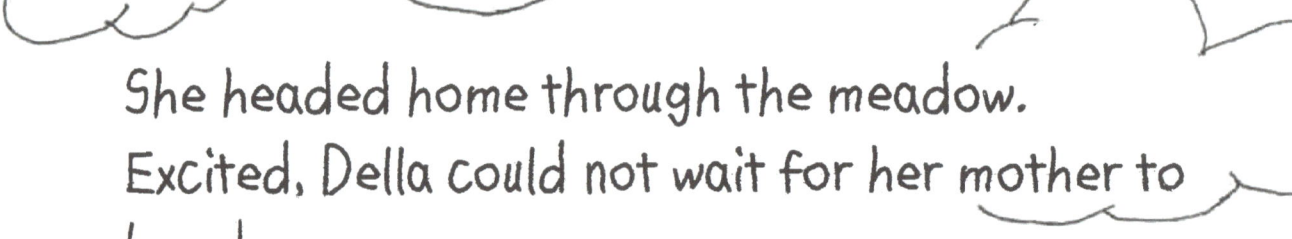

So, she hurried to tell her wonderful dream.
And her garden of flowers and her color scheme.

CPSIA information can be obtained
at www.ICGtesting.com
Printed in the USA
BVHW010718140523
664122BV00006B/51